The Threat of Jihadism in Central Asia

SUMMARY

A. Islamic State and Central Asia

The attacks in Saint Petersburg, Stockholm and Paris on 3, 7 april 2017 & 12 may 2018 respectively have brought to light that the Islamic extremist mindset do not spare citizens from Central Asia states. Perpetrators of these attacks, Akbarjon Djalilov, kirgiz citizen, Rakhmat Akilov, uzbek citizen, and Hassan Azimov, Russian citizen Chechen, were for two of them building sector workers in the countries where they lived; willing to join Syria, they fell down in radicalization in contact with Chechen recruiters or from central Asian diaspora[1].

The implantation of Khorasan[2] state became a real motivation for central asia jihadists; such an extent that IS tries to spread into the region thanks to alliances with Tehreek-I-Taliban[3] in order to unite all the terrorists groups under the flag of IS.

For Central Asian states, the stake is to avoid the coming back of citizens left to Syria and to limit the extremist contagion. Despite of their governance weakness and economic situation, the penetration of IS seems to be complex for social and cultural reasons. Thus, economic migration to Russia, Turkey and to European Union become a privileged target for recruitment.

Study by state will conclude this quick overview.

---

[1] Following attack in Russia, 8 persons have been detained. Their names revealed origin from Central Asia.
[2] Mollah Fazlullah of Pakistanese territories (SWAT) is considering himself as the founder of Khorasan.
[3] 6 chiefs of Tehreek-I-Taliban (TTP) claimed their allegeance to Daech. ISIS in Central Asia, P Stobdan, 22 oct 14, Institute for Defence studies and analyses.

1. Weakness of political governance

Head of Central Asian states are often seen as authoritarian regimes even leaded by real autocrats: the political speech of the former Uzbek head of state M. Karimov or the way to manage political affairs in Tajikistan are some examples. In parallel, political systems remain closed (around 90 to 99% for election polls).

Local citizens and NGO often denounce nepotism and corruption. In Uzbekistan, a police reform has been initiated in order to make it less open to the corruption and to the political abuse[4]. During the Constitution day, the new Uzbek president M. Mirziyoyev has made a statement concerning the transparency inside the Ministry of Internal Affairs and announced the creation of complaint's mechanism in case of abuse. It was a long-time demand from the population.

Certain tension inside the population is also due to the political marginalization of some specific ethnic groups, as the Shiite in Tajikistan. The incidents in Ferghana Valley are one of the consequences. Sometimes political actions also fan the ambers. The part of population sharing extremist religious point of view has increased from 1% - engaged islamists – and 10% of observers in 2010, to 2% and 15% respectively in 2016[5].

The economic context in Central Asia is quite bad and the low raw material prices have crippled national budgets. The population average in Central Asia with less than 1,25 $ by day is close to 10% (only the Kazakhstan shows a better rate in the area)[6]. High emigration is revealing of the economic stagnation: 4 millions of people from Central Asia are working abroad, especially in Russian Federation[7].

---

[4] Eurasianet.org, « Police Reform is on the way », 8 décember 2016.
[5] Interview of René Cagnat, L'humanité Magazine, 11 august 2016.
[6] Policy Papers, ISIS and its Presumed Expansion into Central Asia, No 19, Juin 2015, Polish institute of international affairs.
[7] ISIS in Central Asia, P Stobdan, 22 oct 14, Institute for Defence studies and analyses,

The economic context, ethnic tensions and the lack of governance to manage problems increase radical religious behaviors in the area: in Kirgizstan, in 1991, there were only 39 mosque and 1000 illegal ones and nowadays there are around 2000[8]. . In March 2016, the Bulan institute for Peace innovations published a report indicating that Kirgiz madrasas are operating without receiving state authorization[9]. The government uses the threat of radicalization in order to take repressive measures against minority (for example, the limitation of civil rights of Uzbek minority in Kirgizstan).

Fighting the extremist threat spreading its south flank, Russian Federation brings a military support to Central Asian states. During the summit of Commonwealth of Independent States in Astana in 2017, the president V. Putin proposed to his counterparts to create joint units of border guards to manage potential crisis[10].

It remains that IS has not really succeeded to develop itself in the area for multiple reasons we will review.

2. Résistance et influence

Central Asia is far from being the first area for recruiting jihadists, even if the Russian president V. Putin has spoken of 5000 to 7000 warriors coming from former USSR (including Caucasus area) left for jihadism in Middle East or Afghanistan[11]. Some of these warriors in Afghanistan located near the border of Turkmenistan and Tajikistan have been considered as much more major threat than the ones left to Iraq or Syria. Indeed, the former Islamic movement of Uzbekistan, strong of 1000 warriors relocated in Afghanistan, has announced its allegiance in 2014 to IS and conducted operations in the area[12]. On July 24

---

[8] Interview of René Cagnat, L'humanité Magazine, 11 august 2016.
[9] Four madrasas have been closed in april 2017 in Kirgizstan.
[10] 26 Turkmen soldiers died at border with Afghanistan.
[11] Number of jihadists left for Afghanistan are under the banner of Islamic Movement of Turkestan.
[12] Policy Papers, ISIS and its Presumed Expansion into Central Asia, No 19, June 2015, Polish institute of international affairs.

2018, the chairman of the State Border Service of Kirghizstan, U. Sharsheyev, has reported that difficulty grows to tighten the mountain areas borders.

 However, the attack in Saint Petersburg as the recent murders and attacks could announce a shift in their strategy[13].

Concerning the departure of citizens to Middle East, the brigade Shishani Jamaat, leaded by a Chechen is widely known for welcoming volunteers from former USSR. We can find also others groups like the Jamaat Adama, Jamaat Akhmada, the Abu Kamil Dagistanis and the Central Asian jihadi[14].

Carte des pays d'Asie Centrale

Despite of the withdrawal of ISAF from Afghanistan, the hesitated attitude of the new American administration and the geopolitical ambition of Russia and China concerning their respective influence zones, the area remains important especially for raw materials.

Western assistance is focusing on intelligence's sharing, necessary for managing terrorist threats. Moreover, the USA implemented National Defense Authorization Act, section 1004, to support foreign forces struggling with drug trafficking and international organized crime. Special units are in charge of offered training. In 2016, have been budgeted the military training of 1157 of

---

[13] On February 17, IS claimed the attack against russian millitary base in Chechenia ; On1st April 2017, IS claimed the murder of two cops in south of Russia.

[14] ISIS in Central Asia, P Stobdan, 22 oct 14, Institute for Defence studies and analyses.

foreign soldiers[15]. During the last two years, the Tajiks forces have been the most supported. However, the expense commitment for us military aid towards central Asian states have been reduced from 294 M$ in 2012 to 115 M$ in 2015. The resistance of democratic regime in Kirghizstan and the new politic context in Uzbekistan after the death of former president Karimov, could be opportunities for CENTCOM (United States Central Command)[16].

The Russian Federation is involving in the area through Collective Security Treaty Organization (CSTO) to guarantee the borders' security by joint military forces and intelligence' sharing. Besides, more than the terrorist threat on the soil of Russian Federation, it is possible that radicalized migrants from Central Asia would operate more likely in their own countries than in the Middle East: this is what Russia and Central Asian states try to preventBy now, Central Asia does not seem to be a priority for IS: allegiance of former Islamic movement of Uzbekistan has been ignored from 2014, and there is no evidence of wills to create a real Khorasan state. No mention of area into the communication links except the movie on radical Kazakhs children training with guns[17] or the video on a former Tadjik military Special Forces leader joining IS[18]. It is quite understandable that IS tries to appeal to in first sight people from Middle East and Europe with Mediterranean themes (colonization, Israel problem, raw materials plundering).

Following recent attacks in Russia, Sweden and France, migrations from Central Asia, already source of tensions will draw attention. On 4th and 5th of April 2017, for one of his first visits abroad, the president Uzbek M. Mirziyoyev went to Moscow to discuss the economic migration[19]. Contrary to his predecessor who qualified migrant workers as idlers and a shame for entire Uzbek people, the actual president seems to involve in a clarification of economic migration process, especially for the short-term jobs in Russia. Central bank of Russia stated that the money transfers from Russia to Uzbekistan reached a level of 2,74 billions of dollars in 2016[20]. 44% of work permit delivered in Russia during

---

[15] Eurasianet.org, US boosts special Forces training in Central Asia, april 2016.

[16] Eurasianet.org, US boosts special Forces training in Central Asia, april 2016.

[17] www.dailynews724.com/race-towards-good-isis-chilling-video-of-kids-using-guns-webtv,37578.html

[18] « Glava OMON Tadzhikistana prisyagnul na vernost Islaskomu gosudarstvu", Moskovskiy Komsomolets, 28 may 2015

[19] Uzbek public relations' presidency.

[20] Central Bank of Russia, report on foreign money transfers, march 2017.

year 2016 have been issued towards Uzbek citizens. From the independence in 1991, almost all the Central Asian states have known a high economic migration to Russia Federation or Turkey in a minor destination[21]. . However, it is important to point out that the majority of migrant workers are not receptive to go for the jihad in IS territories, as they are struggling for a work permit[22] and sending almost all their salaries to their families left at home.

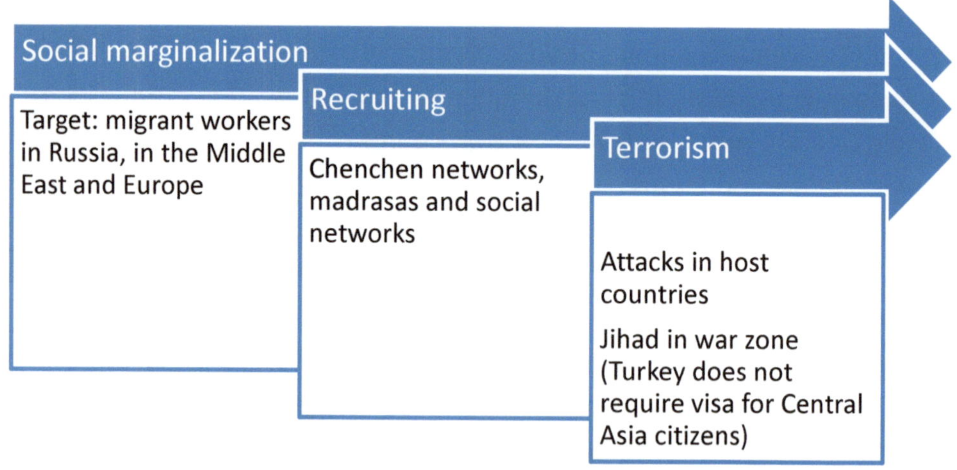

The living standard of population in Central Asia remains low and Investments in health and education fields are weak (133th position for Tajikistan in education field; the winner is Kazakhstan with a 70th position). People are emigrating because of difficulties to live decently but are not falling into the trap of radicalization process. So far, there is not an obvious link between poverty (or even autocratic governance and involvement for extremism ideas. Moreover, the low use of internet among population is an obstacle for IS recruiting in the area.

Religion in Central Asia is in majority Sunni Islam (83% Sunni Muslims, 5% Shia Muslims). Area was widely influenced by Sufi sodality: the mausoleum of the founder of Naqshbandi order is located near Bukhara (Uzbekistan) where he

---

[21] Policy Papers, ISIS and its Presumed Expansion into Central Asia, No 19, June 2015, Polish institute of international affairs.

[22] Sakharovo, near Moscow, is an important center for work permit certification, especially for uzbek workers.

was born in XIVth century. However IS rhetorical is not efficient for two reasons:

- Shiite are constituting a minority only in south of Tajikistan
- Conceptually, thoughts' schema of population of Central Asia are far from Middle East issues or even from pan Islamic ideology.

3. Development axis and solutions

The homeland security of area involves all the regional players, which, through multinational organizations, bring their support in different fields. To fight the terrorism and criminal groups, United States and European Union have launched several economic aid programs and development programs, which need to be continued.

India seems to involve herself, especially in Afghanistan. For her, Russian or Turkish tongue terrorists are not a threat but the issue could be appear if connections are done with Kashmir groups.

Russia as Iran could offer their economic support for a quality religious education in Central Asia. The current religious education given by madrasas turned out not efficient for work market.

China is settling enormous construction sites in order to buy social peace with the full employment, especially towards young generations[23]. In the frame of the new Silk Road, opportunities offer to China to develop exponentially their economic investments, in particular in the field of facilities. China is seeking also to reduce potentially threat of Uighur minority through the border. However, some issues remain as China relies on a Chinese low qualified work labor[24].

---

[23] Unemployment rate is relatively low : in Tajikistan, 2,50% and in Kirghizstan, 8,60 %

[24] In 2010, some kirghyz clans of At Bachi region are gone to war riding horses against settlement of chinese company which wanted to extract gold from a mine dedicated to kirghiz for long time ago.

In order to prevent any native extremist process among population, it remains urgent to increase nation- building process and to support reforms, as the police's in Uzbekistan in 2017. The rural administration should be structured and reformed with support of foreign joint programs; at the same time, clan-based links should be reinforced[25].

In conclusion, until 2018 the central Asian terrorism linked directly to IS tends to spread among Diasporas weakened by an adverse socio-economic context in their host country. Remains the issue of coagulation of different native terrorist groups, which could create a real threat for central Asian states. The last events in Tajikistan concerning the killing of four foreign cyclists could announce a shift in Islamic State strategy: exporting terrorism directly thanks to former jihadists back in their own countries.

---

[25] Projects in Tajikistan, Solidarity Fund, www.solidarityfund.pl/en/opisy-projektow-2013/wg-krajow-2/tadjikistan

4. Study case by countries

> Comparison of leaving for jihad by countries with some Middle East or European countries

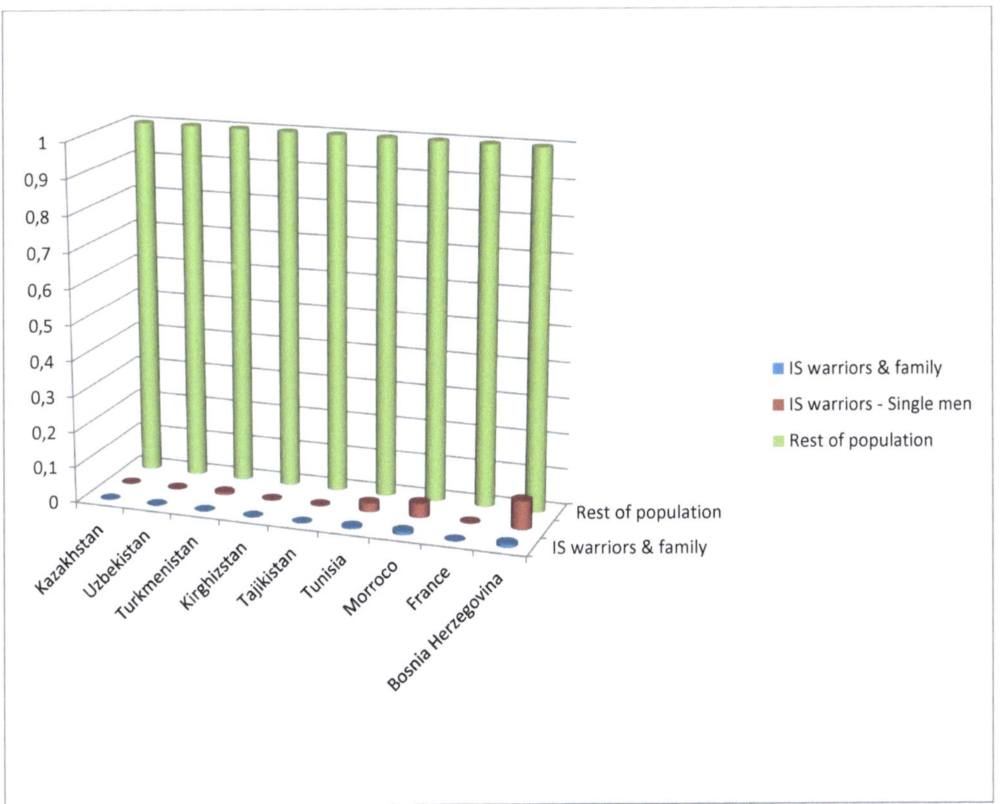

In Kazakhstan, volunteers to jihad are Salafist and not Hanafi. The Tablighi Jammat is the major recruitment group in the area.

In Kirghizstan, volunteers are often single men and without criminal background.

In Tajikistan, volunteers are often from the same villages, or from the same clan. Most of them have been killed in Syria and Iraq. On attack of four cyclists in July 29 2018 in the country, some of the suspected conspirators came from the same village, Nurek.

Volunteers from Uzbekistan are joining the Jabhat Al-nosra group and more recently the former IMU.

➢ Motivations of jihadists from Central Asia

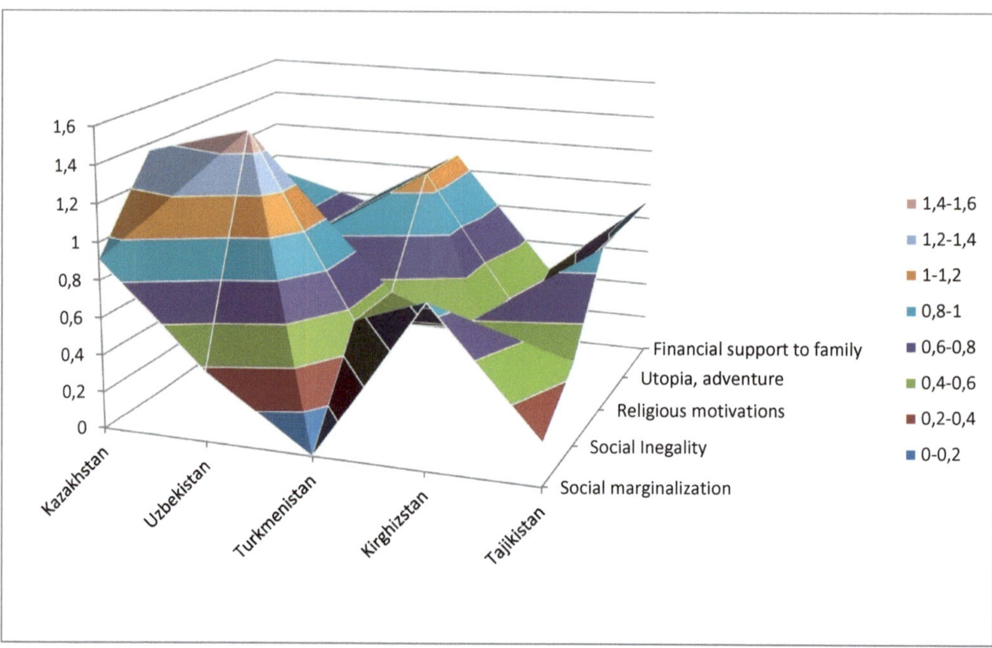

In Kazakhstan, radicalization on the disparity theme is often the scheme of female extremism.

In Kirghizstan, the religious radicalization is built up on the utopia of real Islamic state in the area, and against the repression methods against Uzbek minority in the country.

The Tajikistan is formed on ethnic basis – Sunnite in the west, Shiite in the southeast. The comeback of fighters left for jihad often concludes by strong jail condemnations. IS propaganda can affect some young unemployed people by internet: J. Yusufov is alleged to have participated to attack of July 29 2018 against 4 foreign cyclists (Imam of his hometown, Nurek, has indicated that he was not specially pious).

In Turkmenistan, clan-basis and state identity remain strong. Recruitment is made among marginalized people which weak clan-based links

B. IS-Khorasan, fallback for jihadists from Iraq and Syria?

The word Khorasan is from person and means "from where comes from the sun". In the IS interpretation, it refers to the medieval word of Afghanistan gave by Afghans itself. It included Afghanistan, south of Turkmenistan, Uzbekistan, Tajikistan and the north east of Iran[26].

IS in Khorasan is a wing of IS in Middle East which acts in Afghanistan and Pakistan but his potential operation area stretches up to the Indian subcontinent.

The fall of Mosul precipitated exile of fighters to Afghanistan. The spectra of extremist destabilization threatens Central Asian states because of the proximity of Islamic spot, the porosity of Tajiks borders and the weak governance.

Isis establishment in Afghanistan did not come without clashes, especially among other rebels groups. The current resurgence of attacks shows the will to export the jihadist dynamism in the area. However, some resistance's axis remain.

1. History and evolution of settling in the AfPak area

The declaration of caliphate by Abu Bakr al-Baghdadi in Mosul during the year 2014 drove to some defects of commanders of Tehrir-i-Taliban Pakistan recorded in October 2014, followed by recruitments in Helmand and Farah provinces[27] and allegiance of former IMU. Beginning on January 2015, spokesperson of IS stated the recognition of allegiance by the announcement of creation of Khorasan province (Wilayat Khorasan)[28].

---

[26] Some of cities in this area are famous : Samarkand, Bukhara, Herat ; famous poets : Ansari & Avicenne.
[27] "Islamic State gaining around group in Afghanistan: UN", AFP, 3 october 2014.
[28] "Wilayat Khurasan: Islamic State consolidates position in Afpak region", Jamestown Foundation, 3 april 2015.

The military gain from IMU's allegiance to IS was not relevant – most of defects have concerned fighters pushed back by their commanders, and frustrated by successive defeats recorded by Taliban during the period. In fact, IS has suffered military failures: defeat against Taliban in the Zabul province in Afghanistan during the end of year 2015 and loose of large part of district of Nangarhar and Farah in 2016[29].

The no restriction rule for bombing in early 2016 permitted the increase of targeted strikes by American drones [30] as the famous strike with the "mother of bombs" in Nangarhar on 13th April 2017[31]. Several American strikes have disorganized the high command of IS in Khorasan by death of most of them: defector Taliban Hafiz Saeed Khan dead in 2016, his right-hand man Abdul Rauf Aliza already dead in 2015. Afghan special units with American support have conducted an operation in Nangarhar province which has been concluded by the death of successor of Khan, Sheikh Abdul Hasib, and several IS leaders.

Despite of the military defeats, pockets of resistance lived on in nine provinces. Moreover, attacks perpetrated by IS have increased in 2016: terrorist dynamism could supersede military dynamism.

Last territory losses of IS in Iraq and Syria could increase importance of Afghanistan for the group.

Terrorist attacks by IS in Khorasan during years 2016 and 2017 in Afghanistan and Pakistan.

---

[29] "Wilayat Khorasan stumbles in Afghanistan", Jamestown Foundation, 3 march 2016; "The islamic movement of Uzbekistan comes unraveled", Radio Free Europe/RL, 28 november 2015.
[30] "Air strikes hit Islamic state in Afghanistan under new rules:US", Reuters, 14 april 2016.
[31] Strike with GBU43/B MOAB bomb has been done in Nangarhar district in order to destroy terrorist complex on 13 april 2017.

Terrorist attacks by Islamic State in Khorasan in Afghanistan and Pakistan for 2016 until 2018

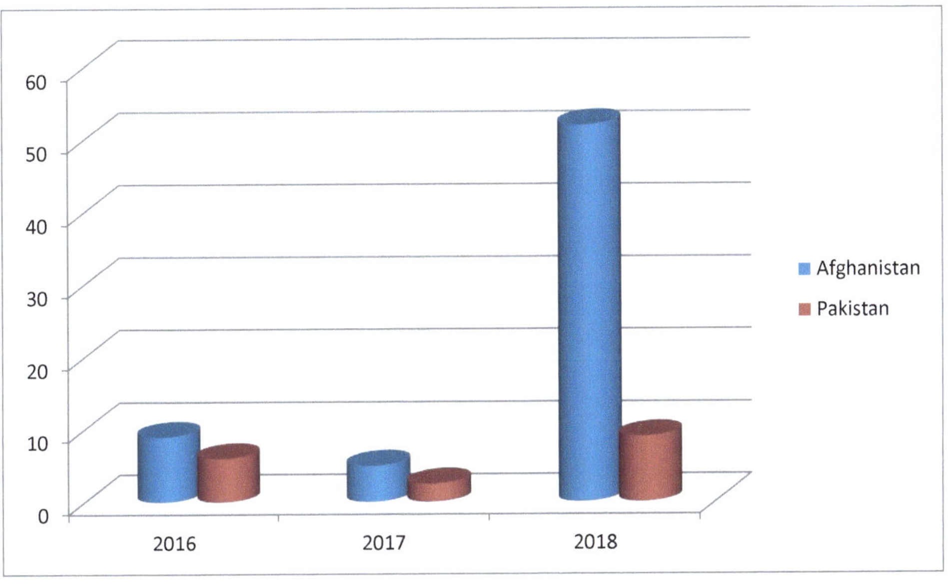

2. AfPak area, source of income and fallback for jihadists

The slow recognition by the afghan government of the IS threat hanged over realistic appreciation, reinforced by the attempts from Taliban to negotiate[32], Multiplicity of terrorist and rebel groups in Pakistan[33] play a great role in uncontrolled spreading of IS inside the country. With its ups and downs, IS remained in the area from 2015, even competed with Talibans, in Sangin for example[34].

Besides, Afghanistan became source of income for IS: heroin trafficking provides to the group billions of dollars[35]. . As hydrocarbon trafficking from Syria to Turkey has been stopped and racket resources narrowed because of territories losses, drugs trafficking became essential for the financial sake of IS. Nevertheless, the limited territory controlled by IS in Afghanistan is not sufficient to develop exportation roads of heroin.

The transfer attempt of Middle East conflict to Afghanistan became an evidence following attacks against Iraq embassy in Kabul, attack against Shiite mosque in Herat in July 2017 and attack of 4 cyclists in Tajikistan in 2018. Number of afghan officials, especially the afghan ministry of defense general Dawlat Waziri, have raised issue of thousands of foreign fighters fled from Syria, under the flag of IS in Nangarhar[36]. United States have shown wills to involve more to prevent IS settling.

However, it is possible that the announcement of IS fighters fled from Syrian settlements into troops ranks of IS in Khorasan, is only a propaganda operation, despite reality here and there: in fact, the attack against Iraq embassy was claimed by IS and attackers were identified as Abu Julaybib al-Kharasani et Abu Talha-Balkhi, Arabs names but with afghan origin. In his own country, J.

---

[32] These attempts could have been pushed some warriors into Islamic State.

[33] Pakistan has a lot of foes : al-Qaeda, Haqqani network, Taliban in the north of the country, Kachmir rebels & IS in Khorasan.

[34] Sangin has been a famous resistance point by Taliban against afghan & foreign forces. Nowadays, IS-K is assumed to be present in the area, Independent UK, mars 2015.

[35] Viktor Ivanov, chief of Russian Federal Service on control of drug trafficking provide a statement of 1 billion which could be surestimated.

[36] Afghan government press , july 2017.

Yusufov, tajik citizen, is alleged to have participated to attack of July 29 2018 against 4 foreign cyclists[37].

3. IS-Khorasan, regional stake

The consolidation of IS in Khorasan, utopic or real, is a real stake for the states bordering Afghanistan because it highlights the group which contains some of their citizens. The former Islamic Movement of Uzbekistan, strong of one thousand fighters, relocated in Afghanistan, had declared its allegiance to IS in year 2014.[38].

The wish to establish a real "Khorasan state" in the area will become a major risk upon arrival destination of fighters fled from Syria. Jihadists from Uzbekistan or Kirghizstan should prefer to stay in IS in Afghanistan and not in their own countries as they could face heavy jail penalties even if some are trying. In 2017, the GKNB, State committee for National Security of Kirgizstan, has announced that on instructions from IS leaders, one citizen left for jihad has reentered in the country in order to form a terrorist cell composed of people who has arrived from conflict areas in Syria[39].

Nepotism, corruption, as politic marginalization of some ethnic groups weakens social basis of countries.

In the same time, Central Asian terrorism linked to IS has tended to spread surfing on diaspora, but has no succeeded to establish itself in the area; the current rising of issue of fallback in Khorasan will depend on coagulation between several terrorist groups with IS.

---

[37] Video of Islamic State published on official website of IS, july 31 2018.
[38] Policy Papers, ISIS and its Presumed Expansion into Central Asia, No 19, June 2015, Polish institute of international affairs.
[39] GKNB, Report of July 19 2018.

C. Come back of jihadists in South Asia, spectra of civil war

Following the fall of IS in Iraq and Syria in 2017, the comeback of jihadists in their own countries became an issue. However, the jihadist dynamism does not concern only former members of IS: in Tunisia, which has a huge number of citizens in IS group, M. Bhiri, former Minister of Justice, claimed in February 2017 for the opening of investigation on Tunisian citizens.

In South Asia, and more particular in Afghanistan and Tajikistan because of jihadist networks, redeployment of IS would be a real threat for regional governance by its radical speech and training capabilities of other terrorist groups.

2018 has already become a horrible year for attacks in Afghanistan. For other hand, comeback of Shiite brigades involved in the support of Syrian regime indicative of a virtual status of civil war.

1. War escalation of Sunnite terrorists groups

Since 2001, the conflict built itself around the struggle between afghan government supported by western armies and Taliban groups and allies.

Weakness of afghan state [40] state – corruption, political rivalry and institutional blocking– reinforced destabilization of the country, letting large part of the effective governance of major regions to Taliban (they would control around 30-40% of the rural part).

The delay of legislative polls since 2016 to July 2018, due to the lack of parliamentary majority to vote the new electoral law, is going against population.

Economically speaking, drugs trafficking issue aside, entropy of the government jeopardizes its capabilities, which has to lean on foreign investments: for example, the building of railroad from Hairatan hairbor on Amou-Daria to the Pakistanis border at Turkhan by a Chinese consortium for 10 billions of dollars[41].

Socially speaking, Taliban are well settled among the rural population. However, the fall of caliphate of IS in Iraq and Syria brought the issue of settlement's recalibration of jihadists in Afghanistan. Some Chechens, Tajiks, North African and French IS leaders are assumed to have already reached Afghanistan's terrorists camps in small number.

Like a loose cannon, IS is trying to recruit inside the afghan educated middle class, and into universities particularly. Salafist indoctrinating would trigger more specifically city dweller. IS cells have been in activity in south and east of the country.

---

[40] Afghan governement was leaded by a coalition around the afghan president, pachtoune, and the first minister, Abdullah Abdullah, tajik.
[41] See AFP.

Extremist actions taken by IS have increased the attacks in the country from beginning of 2018.

Attacks perpetrated by IS Khorasan and Taliban and number of victims

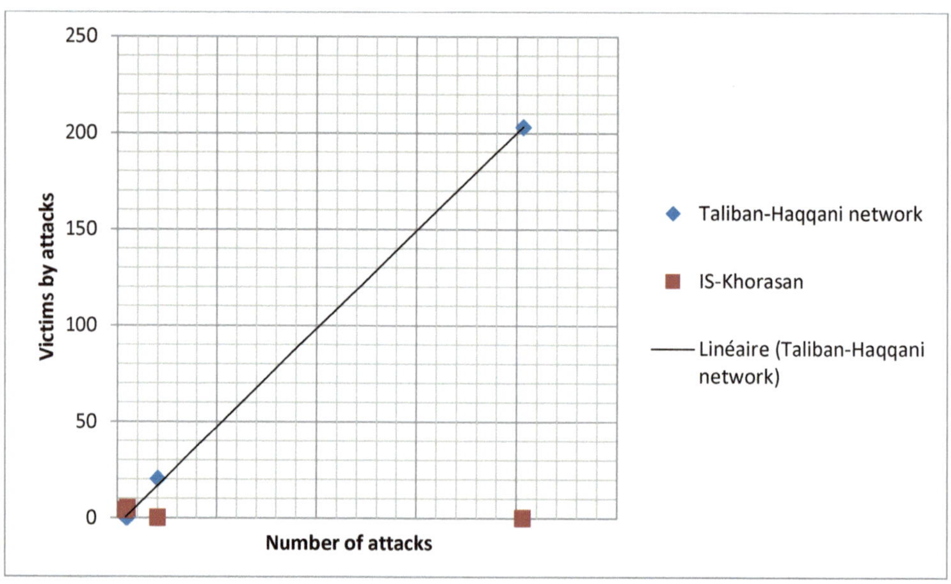

Some attacks in 2018 :

- 20 january : Claimed by taliban. Intercontinental hostel of Kabul, 20 dead
- 25 january : Claimed by IS-Khorasan. ONG save the children in Jalalabad, 5 killed
- 27 january: Claimed by Haqqani network. Ambulance bomb in Kabul, 203 dead
- 28 january : Claimed by IS-Khorasan. Military Academy of Kabul, 5 dead
- 22 april 2018 : IS suicide bomber in party : 48 Shiites killed et 112 wounded
- 4 june 2018 : IS suicide bomber against religious leaders, 4 dead

Almost twenty terrorist groups are operating inside Afghanistan. The sake of High Council for Peace opened since 2010 and its incapacity to negotiate peace with Taliban symbolizes the failure front of attacks increase. Nevertheless, only a minority (5 to 10%) of the population would applause the return of Taliban at the head of the country.

Germs of civil war seem to loom because of rivalry of Sunnite terrorist groups, struggle for power at the head of afghan government, American strategy that would make the best of status quo and the Pakistanis play in the support of Haqqani network. To this explosive situation, Shiite jihadists lays it on thick.

2. Threat of Shiite jihadists coming back from Syria

Survival of Syrian regime is due to Russian involvement in the conflict, but also from the Iranian involvement by mercenaries sending. It is part of a great geopolitical game between Saudi Arabia and Islamic Republic of Iran. To counter Iran, Saudi Arabia has given to Dushanbe over than 200 million of $'s aid.

With the relative withdrawal of thousands of Shiite mercenaries from the front in Syria after the fall of Islamic State and decline of Sunni rebels groups except Kurds, the comeback of jihadists could happen; and among them[42], there are Shiite afghan brigades, especially Fatimid brigade which consists of afghan hazaras (Shiite) with some Tajiks Shiite fighters. The total number of fighters would be around 15 000, a lot more than the 5 000 "volunteers" of IS.

Nevertheless, Iranian supervision was necessary because of the unpreparedness of them unable to plunge into frontline and serving a long time as cannon fodder[43].

It could be established a parallel between jihadists from one side to another: strong ideological footprint, youth and a vague will to question borders issued of divisions from years 1920. Utopia against Utopia: new Islamic city against Arabic unity[44].

Political interests of Syrian government have reached religious faith of Shiite mercenaries based on the defense of sacred Shiite sites against Sunnite[45]. Some experts explain it by pecuniary or social advantages – to gain a work

---

[42] To be note that existing some Sunnite jihadist, in a minority position, who fighted and still fight for syrian regime, as the arab nationalist guard (GNA).

[43] A leader of the brigade, Zohair Mojahed, claimed 2000 killed inside his troops, AFP, 6 january 2018.

[44] Nationalinterest.org, « Shia in Syria », october 2016.

[45] In Damas, we can find the tomb of grand daugther of Muhamad (Sayyida Zaynab).

permit or residence permit in Iran for afghan refugees-[46] – but videos showing, on social networks, fighters of these brigades reciting the Fatiha, first Sourate of Koran, confirm ideological thesis of their motivations[47].

Moreover, the fact that dozens of thousands Shiite Indians have shown strong interest to go to fight for Karbala and Najaf threatened by IS in 2014, is another example of ideological footprint of this conflict spreading in south Asia[48].

Motivations of Jihadists involved with Syrian regime

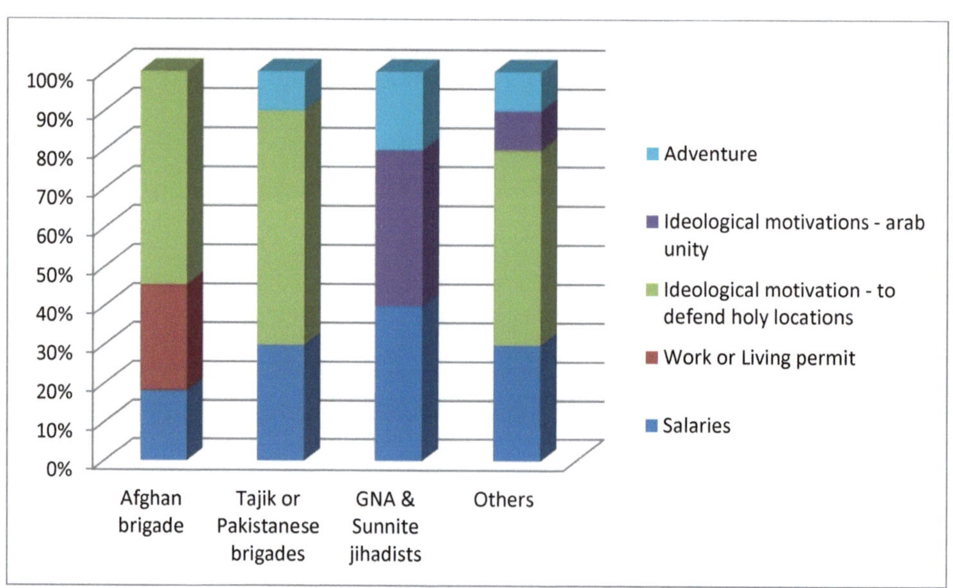

Iranian proselytism in South Asia has widely spread promoted by pull factor created by the conflict to recruit Shiite mercenaries: several internet websites in Urdu language have been used to recruit Shiite of Tajikistan and Pakistan to jihad[49].

Iranian influence in the area has been supported by the opening of religious schools in South Asia since 2011 and the creation of a liaison office of

---

[46] Wall street Journal, « Afghans from Iran forced to go to Syria » décember 2017.
[47] Salaries offered into Shiite brigades are less than 4 times fois compared to those of Islamic State.
[48] Ibtimes.uk, june 2014.
[49] Telegraph.co.uk, february 2015.

Hezbollah in Afghanistan and Pakistan. Popular initiatives in villages have been organized – politics against Zionism but also against Saudi Wahhabism: this kind of initiative has however more success in Middle East than in South Asia.

With the comeback in their own countries of jihadists Shiite (even if Hezbollah captures a large part of fighters in Middle East), the issue of Iranian influence in Afghanistan and in Pakistan would arise. The formation of task forces trained and supervised into its influence area from Liban to South Asia has been liable to recriminations from USA and some western countries: that is how we should understand the speech given by French foreign affairs ministry, M. Le Drian in early 2018[50].

Tajik government used the recent attack on July 29 2018 in Tajikistan against foreign cyclists to accuse banned Islamic Renaissance Party of Tajikistan to be under this terrorism act[51]. The suspected dead leader of this plot, Abdusamadov, was supposed to have been trained in a terrorist camp in Iran – a Shia dominated nation where the Islamic State has not any settlement. Foreign ministry of Iran has denied any connection between Iran and this plot[52].

In a tough context, the redeployment of IS-Khorasan, radicalization of Taliban, American hesitation and inefficient Pakistanis and afghan governments have brought to an edge religious rivalry between Sunnite and Shiite. In the image of Pakistan teared up during years 1980 by religious antagonism, situation status is critical [53].

However, despite of Iranian wills to maintain the control over its mercenaries once back in their own countries, it will be difficult to prevent that links slacken.

---

[50] « No to Iran mediterranean axis », Reuteurs, 12 december 2017.
[51] A court in Tajikistan has sentenced 14 people of this party to jail (7 to 26 years in prison), Eurasianet.org, 2018/08/02.
[52] Mehr news agency, 31 July 2018.
[53] Nationalinterest.org, « Shia in Syria », october 2016.